HEINEMANN HISTORY

USING HISTORICAL SOURCES

IAN COLWILL
Former Chief Examiner, LEAG

CHRIS CULPIN
Chief Examiner, LEAG

COLIN SHEPHARD
Director, Schools History Project,
Chief Examiner, MEG

PAUL SHUTER
Chief Examiner, SEG

Heinemann Educational,
a division of Heinemann Educational Books Ltd,
Halley Court, Jordan Hill, Oxford OX2 8EJ

OXFORD LONDON EDINBURGH
MADRID ATHENS BOLOGNA PARIS
MELBOURNE SYDNEY AUCKLAND SINGAPORE TOKYO
IBADAN NAIROBI HARARE GABORONE
PORTSMOUTH NH (USA)

First published 1990
        95 11 10 9 8 7 6 5

British Library Cataloguing in Publication Data

Using historical sources.
1. Historical sources
I. Colwill, Ian
907

ISBN 0-435-31045-3

Produced by Visual Image, Street, Somerset

Printed in Great Britain by
Scotprint Ltd, Edinburgh

Acknowledgements

The authors and publisher would like to thank the following for
permission to reproduce the following photographs:

English Heritage: 2.6A;
Express Syndication Picture Library: 2.3E;
Kitty Hart: 2.5F;
Hulton-Deutsch: 3.8B, 3.9A;
Illustrated London News Picture Library: 3.4A;
Imperial War Museum: 1.1A, B and C, 2.3C and D, 2.4C, 2.5E, 3.4B
and D, 3.6A and B, 3.7A;
London Transport Museum: 3.11B;
The Mansell Collection: 3.7B;
National Museum of Ireland: 1.3B;
Peter Newark's Pictures: 2.4A and B;
Novosti Picture Library: 3.9B;
Christopher Oxford: 2.4E and F;
Popperfoto: 2.1D, 2.4D, 3.11A and C;
Scott Polar Research Unit, Cambridge: 3.3A;
Society for Cultural Relations with USSR: 3.9C;
Gordon Thomas and Max Morgan-Witts/Jonathan Clowes: 3.10A
and C;
University of Reading, Institute of Agricultural History and
Museum of English Rural Life: 1.3A;

The photograph which appears in 3.12E is taken from *Der Tod des
Adolf Hitler (The Death of Adolf Hitler)* by Lev Bezymenski, copyright
© 1968 by Harcourt Brace Jovanovich Inc., reprinted by permission
of the publisher.

Cover photographs by the Imperial War Museum.

We have been unable to trace the copyright holder of 2.5C and
would be grateful for any information that would enable us to do so.

We are grateful to the following for permission to reproduce
material which originally appeared in examination papers:
London East Anglian Group; Midland Examining Group; Southern
Examining Group; Southern Regional Examinations Board.

Details of Written Sources

In some sources the wording or sentence structure has been
simplified to make sure that the source is accessible.

Ziggi Alexander and Audrey Dewjee, *The Wonderful Adventures of
Mrs Seacole in many lands*, Falling Wall Press, 1984: 3.2A, B, C, D, E
and F
L. Bezymenski, *The Death of Adolf Hitler*, Harcourt Brace
Jovanovich, 1968: 3.12E
Apsley Cherry-Garrard, *The Worst Journey in the World*, Penguin,
1922: 3.3C
Felix Greene (Ed.), *Time to Spare*, Allen & Unwin, 1935: 3.8C
Peter Haining, *The Mystery and Horrible Murders of Sweeney Todd,
Demon Barber of Fleet Street*, Muller, 1979: 3.1B, D and E
T. Harrison and C. Madge (Eds.) *Britain by Mass Observation*,
Century Hutchinson, 1986: 3.8E
H. G. Hibbert, *Playgoer's Memories*, Grant Richards, 1920: 3.1D
C. A. R. Hills, *The Fascist Dictatorships*, Batsford, 1979: 2.5B
Roland Huntford, *Scott and Amundsen*, Hodder & Stoughton, 1979:
3.3B, D and E
G. Kitson Clarke, *The Making of Victorian England*, Methuen, 1965:
2.2C
Michael Moss and Andrew Forrester (Eds.), *Britain from Waterloo to
the Great Exhibition*, History Broadsheets, Heinemann Educational,
1975: 2.1C
Siegfried Sassoon, *Memoirs of an Infantry Officer*, Faber, 1930: 3.4F
Thomas Shapter, *The History of the Cholera in Exeter in 1832*, 1849:
1.2E
Stuart Sillars, *Women in World War I*, Macmillan, 1987: 3.6C,
D and E
Colin Simpson, *Lusitania*, Longman, 1972: 3.7C, D E and F
Albert Speer, *Inside the Third Reich*, Weidenfeld & Nicolson, 1970:
2.5E
B. A. Steward, quoted in *Flashback: War and Pacifism*, National
Extension College, 1983: 3.4E
David Taylor, *Mastering Social and Economic History*, Macmillan,
1988: 1.2A
Hugh Thomas, *The Spanish Civil War*, Aaron Spottiswood 1961:
3.10B
Robert Westall, *Children of the Blitz*, Penguin, 1987: 2.3A and B
The Diary of Anne Frank, Contact (Amsterdam), 1947: 2.5A

CONTENTS

1.1 UTILITY – WHAT MAKES A SOURCE USEFUL?

When historians find a source there are three basic questions they have to answer:

Is it useful?

Is it primary or secondary?

Is it reliable?

The answers to all three questions are linked. So much so that they often need to be answered at the same time rather than one after the other. The first three Units of this book concentrate on these three questions. You must remember that it is not usually sensible to think about one without also thinking about the other two.

You can only decide whether a source is useful or not in the light of what you want to know. This is obvious. It is also true about the answer to the other two questions. Sources are primary or secondary, and reliable or not reliable, depending on what you want to use them for. There is no such thing as a source that is always useful, or always primary, or always reliable.

Although deciding whether a source is useful or not is usually the easiest of the three questions, it is not always straightforward. A source can be useful for what it is obviously about. It can also be

SOURCE A

Women's Army Auxiliary Corps car drivers, Dieppe, 24 July 1917.

useful for other things that can be learnt from it. For example, photographs usually have a lot of information about things in the background. They can also show incidental details like the way people dressed at the time. Finally, the very existence of the source can be useful. Often the fact that the source exists tells us that people thought it was important to make a record of what was happening.

SOURCE B

Women's Army Auxiliary Corps horse trainers. Mules are being taught to 'foot up'. This stopped them from kicking when being harnessed, c. 1917.

SOURCE C

Woman village blacksmith at work, c. 1917.

QUESTIONS

1 Sources A, B, and C were all taken during the First World War.
   a Suggest ten topics for which an historian would find these sources useful.
   b Suggest five topics that an historian of the First World War might be researching for which these sources would not be useful.

2 Would Source C be useful for an historian studying blacksmithing through the ages? Explain your answer.

3 'Source C shows that by 1917 blacksmithing was a trade dominated by women.'
   a Is this true?
   b Does this show that Source C is unreliable and therefore not useful? Give reasons for your answer.

4 Copy each of the following sentences and, for each one, say whether you think it is true or not and why.
   • All sources are either useful or not useful, you just have to work out which type each source is.
   • Each source can tell you a number of different things.
   • Sources are only useful if they are true.

1.2 PRIMARY AND SECONDARY SOURCES

The differences between primary and secondary sources
A simple definition of a primary source is to say it comes from the time the historian is studying. This suggests a secondary source comes from after the time the historian is studying. This is not quite good enough. A better definition of a secondary source is to say that it is a source based on other sources. If you talk about a television programme that you have not seen, but someone has told you about, you would be a secondary source. The most important part of the definition, however, is that it changes depending on what you want to know. A history book written this year about the Battle of Hastings is a secondary source for people studying the battle. It is a primary source, however, for someone studying what historians thought about the battle, or even for studying the sorts of books published this year.

SOURCE A

'Cholera actually frightened people and for a time the casual attitude of "accepting" disease was undermined. This infection appeared to strike at all sections of society - not just the labourers; it also struck with alarming speed. The local Boards of Health tried desperately to control the epidemic. Houses were whitewashed with chlorate of lime and barrels of burning tar were placed in the street to "disperse the miasma".'

From David Taylor, 'Mastering Social and Economic History', 1988.

SOURCE B

Drinking water being collected at the 'Dipping Steps' in Exeter. These steps were bricked up after the cholera epidemic of 1832. From Thomas Shapter, 'The History of the Cholera in Exeter in 1832', 1849.

SOURCE C

Houses in Fore-street, Exeter. Described by Shapter as interesting specimens of old English houses, they were still standing in 1849. From Thomas Shapter, 'The History of the Cholera in Exeter in 1832', 1849.

Why do historians want to know which is which?

Knowing whether a source is primary or secondary does **not** tell you whether it is reliable. It does, however, tell you how to find this out. Primary and secondary sources are checked for reliability in different ways. To check a secondary source for reliability (for example a history of the Second World War) you need to know whether the historian read all the necessary sources before writing it. If the book did not use any German sources it would certainly miss out important things. As well as knowing whether the historian has used the right sources you could always check to see that he or she had used the sources honestly and accurately. Just think how leaving out a little word like 'not' might change the meaning of a quotation. Primary sources are checked for things such as bias, the reason someone had for creating them, whether that person was in a position to know anyway, and so on.

A more important difference

Sources can be categorized in other ways. One of the most useful ways is to think about **why** they were created. Some sources, both primary and secondary, deliberately tell you what you want to find out about. The person who created the source actually thought it would tell people what had happened. The memoirs of a famous person are a good example. Historians call these sources **witting sources**. Other sources were created for different reasons, but can still be used to tell us about what happened. Someone's passport, stamped with the date a person entered a particular country, could be valuable evidence. However, the passport was not made to tell people when and where someone travelled, it was made because countries insist travellers have passports as proof of who they are. Historians call these sources **unwitting sources**.

SOURCE E

'The paving [of the streets] except in the great thoroughfares, consisted of rounded pebbles, locally known as pitching, so arranged as to slope from the sides to the centre of the road, which thus formed the gutter. This, in very nearly all the streets, was the only means whereby the sewage and nuisances of the city were removed.'

A description of the streets of Exeter in 1832 from Thomas Shapter, 'The History of the Cholera in Exeter in 1832', 1849. Shapter was a doctor in Exeter in 1932.

QUESTIONS

1 Is Source A a primary or a secondary source for historians studying the Cholera outbreak of 1832? Give reasons for your answer.

2 Are Sources B and C primary or secondary sources for historians of Exeter? Give reasons for your answer.

3 Is Source E a primary or a secondary source? Give reasons for your answer.

4 Are any of the sources in this unit unwitting sources? Give reasons for your answer.

5 How useful is it for historians to know:
   a which of these sources are primary and which are secondary?
   b which of these sources are witting sources?

SOURCE D

A bill from the papers of the Exeter Board of Health

Exeter, August 11, 1832.

ISAAC SPRATT, City Crier,

		s.	d.
Cried for the gentlemen of the Board of Health to obtain nurses for the Cholera patients		1	6
Ditto second time		1	6
		3	0

1.3 **RELIABILITY OF SOURCES**

Historians are interested in using sources to find out things about the past. No source is reliable or unreliable. A source is reliable or unreliable when it is used to say something about the past. Just as whether a source is primary or secondary, or whether it is useful or not depends on what you want to know, whether a source is reliable or not also depends on what you want to know. Consider Source A, for example. If you want to know about Victorian painting, this example of a Victorian painting is a useful source. If you are writing about the subjects chosen by painters it is a primary source. If you said, on the basis of this source, that all Victorian paintings were about life in the countryside then your use of the source would not be reliable. If, however, you were collecting statistics about the most popular subjects for Victorian paintings, and you added one to your 'countryside' total on the basis of this painting, then your use of the source would be reliable.

ACTIVITY

Can you work out a series of possible enquiries for an historian for which Source A would be:

- useful, primary, and reliable;
- not useful;
- useful, secondary, and reliable;
- useful, primary, and not reliable;
- useful, secondary, and not reliable?

SOURCE

A farm worker's cottage, painted in the nineteenth century by Mrs Allingham.

SOURCE B

A photograph of a farm worker and his family evicted from their cottage, c. 1880.

SOURCE C

FARM WORKERS

'While many workers in the countryside had a little land of their own, they depended on working on the larger farms to get enough money to live. Their families were poor and needed the money earned by the mother and the children to make ends meet. They would all have to work very hard for long hours and the family could be plunged into poverty by illness or a bad harvest. Farm workers were smaller than the average for the rest of the population. Most farm workers were older when they married, had fewer children, and died younger than the average.'

From a worksheet used in an English school, c. 1982.

EXERCISE

1 What does Source A tell you about the life of farm workers?

2 What does Source B tell you about the life of farm workers?

3 Read the following statements carefully. Say whether you agree or disagree with each one, and give reasons for your answer.
 a None of the people shown in Sources A and B looks thin, so this proves the people in the illustrations had a proper diet.

 b None of the people shown in Sources A and B looks thin, so this proves that most farm workers and their families in the nineteenth century were well fed.

4 Look back at your answers to questions 1 – 3. How does thinking about whether or not the sources are primary, reliable and useful help you answer the questions?

5 The photograph and the painting are primary sources. The written account is secondary. This means the first two sources must be more reliable than the written account. Say whether you agree or disagree and give reasons for your answer.

6 Sources A and B give very different impressions about the life of farm workers in the nineteenth century. Does this mean one of them is useless as historical evidence or could both be useful? Give reasons for your answer.

7 Which of the sources on this page is the most reliable? Give reasons for your answer.

2.1 PROVENANCE AND BIAS

SOURCE A

'Before this system which has corrupted everything in this country, there were none of these places called factories. To speak of them with any patience is impossible. Some of the owners employ thousands of miserable creatures. In cotton spinning they are kept fourteen hours a day locked up, summer and winter, in a heat from 80 to 84 degrees. The rules which they are subjected to are such that no slaves were ever subjected to.'

This was written by William Cobbett, on 20 November 1824. As a source, it tells us almost nothing about factories but a great deal about William Cobbett. Cobbett was famous in his day as a fierce critic of the dreadful living and working conditions of many people in Britain.

1 How can you tell Cobbett hated the factory system?

2 Are there any facts in Source A? If so, do you believe them?

Source A is obviously **biased** (one sided). The point of view of the author has affected the source. An historian, always trying to get at the truth, therefore has to look out for bias in sources.

Sometimes, bias is less obvious; we may read what seems like a straightforward account. But who wrote it? What is its **provenance**?

SOURCE B

'We had this day the pleasure of visiting the workhouse. If chubby smiling faces, and boisterous laughter in the young, and quiet dignity in the old are any test of happiness, content and comfort, and proof of the excellent administration of Mr and Mrs Salmon, they all bear ample witness.'

A description of a visit to Newcastle Workhouse in 1840.

3 If you were trying to find out about life in workhouses in about 1840, how would you use Source B if it had been written by:
- a close friend of Mr and Mrs Salmon?
- someone who was in favour of workhouses?
- someone who was against workhouses?
- a group of middle-class people who were worried about workhouse conditions?

4 Do you think that Source B is an unbiased source?

From your answers to question 1 it is clear that the provenance of a source affects how we use it. Is this still true when we read a source which seems to have only facts, not opinions?

SOURCE C

Q "At what time in the morning did those girls go to the mills?"
A "In the brisk time (ie when they were busy) they have gone about three o'clock in the morning and ended at ten at night."

Q "Had you not great difficulty in awakening your children at this hour?"
A "Yes, in the early time we had to take them up asleep and shake them, and when we got them on the floor to dress them, before we got them off to work."

Q "Were the children excessively fatigued by this labour?"
A "Many times. We have often cried when we have given them the little food we had to give them. We had to shake them and they have fallen asleep with the food in their mouths."

Q "Have your children ever been strapped?"
A "Yes, every one. The eldest daughter, when my wife came in she said her back was beaten nearly to a jelly."

5 These questions and answers are taken from a Parliamentary Committee of 1832. Does that mean that it is unbiased evidence?

6 What impression of factory conditions is given here?

7 Source C consists almost entirely of facts, yet gives a strong impression of factory conditions at the time. How can facts give a biased impression?

8 We know that the Short-Time Committee (a group working to cut factory hours) rehearsed some witnesses in their evidence. How does this further information about provenance affect your view of Source C?

9 Does the further information in question 4 affect your answer to question 1?

SOURCE D

The Strand, London, about 1900.

Even photographs can present problems in how they are used as historical evidence. They are biased and, as with all the sources here, the more information we have on their provenance the better. Look closely at Source D, then answer the following questions.

10 On the basis of Source D, which of the following statements could be made:
   a The Strand was a busy street in 1900.
   b Most people in 1900 wore hats.
   c Horse-drawn vehicles were still very common in London in 1900.
   d Colmans and Nestlés were well-known firms as early as 1900.
   e Motor buses had not been invented by 1900.
   f Street lighting had been invented by 1900.

   g The summer of 1900 was sunny.
   h The technology of photographs was quite advanced by 1900.
   i There was very little traffic control in Britain in 1900.
   j The amount of traffic in London had increased in the 1890s.

11 Which of the statements above can be definitely proved by looking at Source D?

12 Which of the statements above could be proved if we knew more about the provenance of Source D?

13 In what ways does Source D present us with biased evidence?

2.2 **RELIABILITY AND CROSS-REFERENCING**

SOURCE A

'*The March of Bricks and Mortar*', 1829.

A historian trying to find out the truth about the past has to think about the **reliability** of a source. Is the information in it accurate? Does it mean what it says? Is it typical?

Reliability

We have already seen that sources can be biased in different ways. A cartoon is a particular kind of biased source. Source A shows a cartoon by Cruikshank about the growth of cities.

1 In Source A, what are the chimney pots, cement, picks and shovels doing? What are the bricks doing?

2 What are the trees, haystacks and animals doing?

3 How has Cruikshank shown that the houses are badly built?

4 What is Cruikshank's attitude to the growth of cities?

5 Is Source A reliable evidence about the way houses were being built?

6 Is Source A reliable evidence about how people felt about the growth of towns?

You can see that a historian would not use this cartoon as reliable evidence about what is happening in the drawing. It could, however, be used as very reliable evidence about attitudes from around the time it was drawn. You can also see that a source can be both reliable and unreliable, depending on what question is being asked.

Reliability and provenance

We have seen that the most important thing we need to know about a source is its provenance. The reliability of a source for an historian depends on what you can find out about where it comes from.

SOURCE B

'You have to penetrate courts reeking with poisonous gases arising from the piles of sewage and refuse scattered in all directions; courts, many of them which the sun never reaches, which are never visited by a breath of fresh air. You have to climb rotten staircases. you have to grope your way along dark and filthy passages swarming with vermin. Then you may gain admittance to the dens in which thousands of these beings, who belong as much as you to the race for whom Christ died, herd together.'

7 What can you say about the reliability of Source B without knowing any more?

8 Make a list of the qustions you would want answers to in order to establish the provenance, and reliability, of Source B.

9 In fact Source B is an extract from 'The Bitter Cry of Outcast London', written by a minister, Rev. Andrew Mearns, in 1883. Does this information make Source B a reliable or an unreliable source for historians trying to find out about:
● housing conditions in London in the 1880s?
● Rev. Andrew Mearns?
● attitudes to poor housing in the 1880s?

Reliability and primary and secondary sources
Look again at pages 6-7 to refresh your memory about the differences between primary and secondary sources.

SOURCE C

'Suitable housing did not exist and the additional numbers were crammed into every nook and cranny from attic to cellar of old, decaying property, or into cottages run up hastily in confined spaces with little or no access to light and air. Water and sanitation were not provided at all, and where they were provided, there was often a mixture of cesspools and wells.

'Such conditions were not new, nor probably were they worse than what had existed before. But as numbers increased, so these evils increased.'

From 'The Making of Victorian England' by G. Kitson Clarke, published in 1965.

10 Which is more biased in its account of Victorian cities, Source B or Source C?

11 What would you want to know about Source C in order to judge its reliability?

12 Which is the more reliable account of Victorian cities, Source B or Source C?

13 Under what circumstances could a secondary source be **more** reliable than a primary source?

14 Under what circumstances would a secondary source be **less** reliable than a primary source?

Cross-referencing
We can increase our understanding of the reliability of sources by **cross-referencing**. That is, looking for ideas and information which appear in two (or more) sources. In this way we can be more sure of our knowledge, particularly if the sources are quite different.

EXERCISE

1 Look at Sources A, B and C. Copy out the following table. Make a list of statements about housing in Victorian cities which can be made on the basis of more than one source.

Statement	Source A	Source B	Source C
Houses were built quickly	✓	?	✓

2 Does the fact that a statement can be supported by more than one source mean that it **must** be true?

3 Does the fact that some sources have information and ideas which are not supported by any other source here mean that they must be false?

2.3 **INFORMATION OR EVIDENCE ?**

Historians find out about the past from sources of **evidence**. Everything that has survived from the past is a source. This includes letters, clothing, photographs, machines and even the streets, buildings and countryside around us. The historian's job is to find out as much as possible from these sources. At first this may seem a very simple task. Look at Source A. What does it tell you?

We can find out the following things from Source A:

• Rose whispered for days.
• The room was clean.
• The boy had never before cleaned his teeth.

All of this is **information** taken from the source. We have not really had to do much work to get this information. However, if we ask the right questions, this source will give us **evidence** about other things. If we ask: `Was the boy happy to be living in this new place?´ there is evidence in the source which would support the answer that the boy was not happy. In fact, he was quite scared by the strange things around him. When answering questions like this, it is important that you support your conclusion with evidence from the source. What evidence is there in Source A to suggest that the boy was not happy with his new surroundings?

You should note that Source A contains evidence about different kinds of things. It contains evidence about how well the boy was looked after and about his social background. What kind of social background do you think he came from?

The evidence a source gives us depends on the questions we ask about the source. There may be some questions about which the source has no evidence at all. Can you find any evidence in Source A about which city the boy lived in before he was evacuated?

Unfortunately, the information we get from a source cannot always be trusted. Look at Source D. This shows Hitler urging a mother to send her children back to the city. We know that the information in this source (that Hitler spoke to British mothers to urge them to send their children back to the city) cannot be true. Hitler never came to Britain, and certainly never toured the countryside talking to people.

If the information in Source D is not true, does this mean that it is of no use to the historian? Perhaps the source can still be used as evidence. Does it, for example, provide any evidence about German attitudes towards the British evacuation policy? You may think that the source gives us evidence that the Germans wanted British families to go back to the cities so that they could be killed by the bombing. But does Source D give us reliable evidence about this? Remember what we know about the provenance of the source. This poster was drawn to persuade mothers to keep their children in the countryside. The artist may have included Hitler in the drawing as a way of strengthening this message.

It is also worth asking whether Source D provides any evidence about the motives of the British government who employed the artist to draw the poster.

SOURCE **A**

'My sister Rose whispered. She whispered for days. Everything was so clean in the room. We were given face flannels and toothbrushes. We'd never cleaned our teeth until then. And hot water came from the tap. And there was a lavatory upstairs. And carpets. And clean sheets. This was all very odd. I didn't like it.'

A boy, aged 13, writes about being evacuated to the countryside during the Second World War. Many children living in large cities were taken from their homes and sent to live in the countryside where there was much less chance of being bombed.

SOURCE **B**

'After school we were expected to sweep out Mr Benson's butcher's shop and scrub down the marble slabs. I was never asked to help my father in his bank. Once a week we were bathed in a tin bath in front of the fire. We were stripped and scrubbed. Nanny might have approved of the scrubbing, but not of being bathed in the kitchen once a week. Mrs Benson filled us up with thick slices of bread and margarine, just like the bread I used to see our maids eat for their tea. Instead of having to play cricket in the garden, we went bird nesting. One day we dammed up a stream. In the night it flooded the church and six houses.'

A boy, aged 13, writes about his evacuation to the countryside during the Second World War.

SOURCE C

A photograph of children being evacuated during the Second World War.

SOURCE D

DON'T do it, Mother—

LEAVE THE CHILDREN WHERE THEY ARE

ISSUED BY THE MINISTRY OF HEALTH

A poster issued by the British government during the Second World War.

QUESTIONS

1 Who most enjoyed being evacuated the boy in Source A or the boy in Source B? Explain what evidence in the sources you base your answer on.

2 Sources A and B tell us quite a lot about the two boys who wrote them.
  a Write down two things which you discovered from Source A about the boy's way of life before he was evacuated.
  b Write down two things which you discovered from Source B about the boy's way of life before he was evacuated.
  For each answer say which parts of the sources led you to your conclusions.

3 'Source D is of no use to historians because it is only government propaganda.' Do you agree or disagree with this statement? Give reasons for your answer.

SOURCE E

A cartoon published in a British newspaper during the Second World War. The woman is saying to the children: 'Now I want you to promise me you're all going to be really good evacuees and not worry his Lordship'.

4 What could you use Source C as evidence of? Give reasons for your answer.

5 'Source E is not reliable as a source of evidence because cartoons do not tell us what actually happened.' Explain whether you agree or disagree with this statement.

6 Using Sources A, B, C and D write a full account of the evacuation of children during the Second World War.

2.4 PHOTOGRAPHS AS SOURCES

It is often said that 'the camera never lies'. If this is true then surely photographs must be the most valuable type of source the historian has. After all, whatever is shown in a photograph must have been there, exactly as it appears, when the photograph was taken. This means that we can actually see scenes from the past. Sources E and F (page 19) are useful for seeing how the same part of Southport has changed, and Source A shows the horror of war more effectively than words ever could.

Purpose

Photographs, however, have to be used carefully. We know a lot about the American Civil War (1861-5) because it was the first war to be widely photographed. Photography was barely twenty years old and it was not possible to take action shots, or to reproduce photographs in newspapers. But exhibitions of the photographs were staged in New York. One reporter said of these photographs: 'They bring home to us the realities of war. If they do not bring bodies and lay them in our back-yards and along streets, they do something very like it.'

SOURCE **A**

Dead American soldiers, 1862. Photographs like this showed civilians dead Americans after a battle for the first time.

But do these photographs show us the realities of the war? Look at Sources A and B. Do they give the same impression of the war? Do you think that these photographs were taken for the same reason?

The photographer
The very presence of the photographer at the scene can affect what happens. Sometimes people act differently in front of a camera. They may even, for example, invite a photographer and stage a riot just for the camera. Or the photographer may ask them to behave in a certain way. Would the men in Source B normally look like that?

Captions
The caption that goes with a photograph is also very important. If the caption is wrong then the photograph can be misleading. Look at the way a photograph has been used in Source C. If the caption had simply stated that this was the result of a gas explosion, the photograph would be used by the historian in a completely different way.

SOURCE C

A poster issued by the British government during the First World War.

SOURCE B

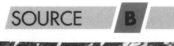

Cavalrymen of the American Civil War. They considered themselves to be an elite.

2.4

Tampering with photographs

Sometimes photographs are altered. Look at Source D. It claims to show three of the Russian leaders, Stalin, Lenin and Kalinin (a supporter of Stalin) in 1919. After Lenin's death in 1924 there was a struggle for power between Stalin and Trotsky. Stalin won and began a campaign to disgrace Trotsky and to make himself appear as Lenin's natural heir. Photographs appeared showing Stalin and Lenin together, but Trotsky was cut out of them. If you look at Source D closely you will see signs that it has been tampered with. Many photographs of this time show Lenin in the same clothes and in the same pose, which should make us suspicious.

SOURCE D

Stalin, Lenin and Kalinin in 1919.

QUESTIONS

1 Look at Sources E and F. What changes have taken place in London Square, Southport, between 1900 and the 1970s?

2 Do you agree that Sources E and F do not tell us much about these changes? Give reasons for your answer.

3 Why do you think the photograph in Source A (page 16) was taken?

4 Does the fact that the photograph in Source B (page 17) was posed mean that it has no use for historians? Give reasons for your answer.

5 Write an alternative caption for the photograph in Source C (page 17) which gives it a completely different meaning.

6 The photograph in Source D has been tampered with. Does this mean that it is not reliable? Give reasons for your answer.

7 'Photographs only show us one moment in time, not what happened before or after. This means they have very limited value for historians.' Explain whether you agree or disagree with this statement.

SOURCE E

London Square, Southport, in 1900.

SOURCE F

London Square, Southport, in the 1970s.

2.5 TYPES OF SOURCES

In some ways the historian studying the recent past is much better off than the historian studying earlier periods of history. The range of source material about the twentieth century is much greater. Can you think why this is? Some types of sources in this book were not produced by earlier societies. Which types are these? Most twentieth-century societies also produce much more source material than earlier societies. Why do you think this is?

The amount of twentieth-century source material also causes problems for the historian. It is impossible to study all the sources now available. It is also difficult to store all of these sources. Governments and other organizations have to make decisions about which sources to keep for historians in the future, and which to destroy. There is always the danger that governments will only preserve sources which they want later generations to see. This probably explains why it is so diffcult to find evidence which links Hitler directly with the mass murder of the Jews. Which sources shown here do you think people involved in the events at the time would have wanted to suppress?

It is sometimes useful to distinguish between sources in terms of their intended audience:

- Sources intended to be private or personal. They were meant to be seen only by the author of the source, or by a few close friends. Examples include diaries, or a letter from a son to his mother.
- Sources produced for the public to see, for example: newspapers, posters, novels and government reports.
- Sources which were not produced for any audience but are simply the product of peoples' lives. It is in this category that most archaeological sources would fall, for example buildings, furniture and clothing. Archaeological sources are usually associated with ancient history but they can be just as important for modern history. Do you agree that archaeological sources were not produced for an audience? Does this mean that all archaeological sources are reliable?

Some types of sources are more useful than others in providing particular kinds of evidence. Sometimes a pictorial source provides us with evidence which a written source could never give us. Written sources, particularly statistics, can often give us very precise evidence that pictures cannot show. Are there any examples of this in the sources here?

SOURCE B

'I visited Treblinka to find out how they carried out their extermination. I did not think their methods very efficient. So at Auschwitz I used a Prussic acid which we dropped into the death chamber. It took from three to fifteen minutes to kill them all. We knew when they were dead because the screaming stopped.'

Rudolf Hoess, commander of Auschwitz extermination camp, speaking during his trial for war crimes in 1946.

SOURCE C

A Nazi poster. Beneath this picture was written 'Communism is the Guardian of Capitalism'.

SOURCE A

11 July 1942	'I can't tell you how horrible it is never to be able to go outdoors and also I am very afraid we shall be discovered and shot.
9 October 1942	I've got terrible news today. Our Jewish friends are being taken away by the dozen. They are loaded into trucks. The English radio speaks of Jews being gassed.
16 September 1943	Relations between us are getting worse all the time. At meals no one dares open their mouths because you either annoy someone or it is misunderstood.'

From the diary of Anne Frank. Anne and her family were Jews and were kept in hiding from the Nazis by friends.

SOURCE D

The number of Nazi votes			German unemployment		
	1928	800,000		1928	1,862,000
	1929	6,400,000		1929	2,850,000
	1930	6,500,000		1930	3,217,000
July	1932	13,700,000	January	1932	6,000,000
November	1932	11,700,000	September	1932	5,102,000

SOURCE F

German girls at a Nazi Party rally.

SOURCE G

The lavatory hut at Auschwitz.

SOURCE E

'Here it seemed to me was hope. Here were new ideals, new tasks. The peril of Communism could be checked and instead of hopeless unemployment, Germany could move towards economic recovery. My mother saw a Storm Trooper parade in Heidelburg. The sight of discipline in a time of chaos, the impression of energy, in an atmosphere of universal hopelessness, won her over.'

Speer, a leading Nazi, describes the attractions of Nazism in his memoirs.

QUESTIONS

1 Do you agree that as Anne did not expect anyone to read her diary (Source A), it is reliable?

2 Hoess was on trial for his life. How reliable is Source B?

3 'Posters like Source C are propaganda and so are of little use to the historian.' Do you agree?

4 Which is the more useful for explaining why Germans supported the Nazis, Source D or Source E?

5 Does Source F tell you anything about Nazi support which you did not already know from Sources D and E?

6 If historians were able to visit the buildings at Auschwitz, what difficulties would there be in using them as evidence?

7 What other types of source, other than those shown here, would be useful in providing evidence about Nazi Germany?

2.6 ARTEFACTS AS HISTORICAL SOURCES

Anything which survives from the past can be a useful historical source. These sources are not only found in museums. Buildings, the things people used in their day to day lives, and even the land itself can help us work out what the past was like.

An artefact is something made by people. A computer, a stone-age flint axe, a house and a bridge are all artefacts. As historical sources they present many of the same problems as all the other types of sources you have met. Obviously they are unlikely to be biased in the same way as sources which try to tell us a story are. This is because sources are not usually created for the same purpose for which they are later used. (This makes them unwitting sources – see page 7). Source A, for example, was not created to tell us about the development of the London Underground. It is part of the underground system, which has been altered at various times. However, we can use the source to tell us something about the story of the system.

What can you work out from the photograph?

The white tiled wall is the wall behind a platform. This, plus the London Underground logo suggest it was part of a tube station. Presumably, the station was not built with an uneven platform, so we may suspect that the platform surface deteriorated over time. At some point it got so bad that a poster was needed to warn passengers. Later still, because they cut across the poster, there were alterations made to this station. A new wall was built and perhaps a new ceiling.

Very often the problems associated with artefact sources are to do with interpretation. We have to spend most of our time working out what the sources are telling us, rather than questioning whether they are reliable or not. However, the conclusions we reach by using artefact evidence are not necessarily perfect. Like any other conclusions in history they are **hypotheses** – the best theories we can develop from the evidence available. If possible, these theories should be tested. Written sources are an obvious place to start. How would the following written sources help you check your explanation of the story behind Source A?

- A map of the underground system listing all the stations.

- The original builders' plans for St Pauls station.

- The records of the department responsible for placing posters in the underground system.

SOURCE A

Photograph of part of St Pauls station, taken c. 1986.

SOURCE B

☞ *The Premium allowed by Oxford Canal Company, must be received by the Purchaser.*

ENSLOW WHARF.

March 1829

Mr. *Smallbone*

Bought of Richard Parker,

	T.	Cw	Qr	£	s.	d.
Gross Weight						
Weight of Carriage ..						
Coke, at per Qr...						
Coals, at per Cwt.	2	–	–	2	11	4
Carriage................						

A document from a local museum.

SOURCE C

Photograph taken in 1990.

SOURCE D

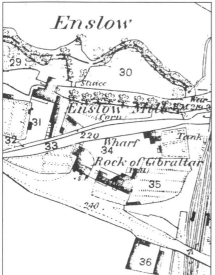

Ordnance Survey map of the area 1875.

EXERCISE

Photographs are a useful way of recording artefact evidence, although they are obviously not as good as studying the real thing.

1 Look carefully at Sources B, C and D. What do you think the building in Source C was once used for? You may find it helpful to consider the following questions:

- What was the original form of the building and what changes have been made to it?

- What does Source D tell you about the area around the building?
- Is there any reason to connect Source B with the building?

2 What other sources might help you test your theory?

3 Do you think your answer is definately true or likely to be true? Explain why.

3.1 SWEENEY TODD, DEMON BARBER

Sometimes historians have to decide whether a story is based on real events or fiction. One such story is that of Sweeney Todd, the so-called 'Demon Barber of Fleet Street'. He is supposed to have robbed and murdered his unsuspecting customers, and then handed their corpses over to his partner in crime, a Mrs Lovett, who made them into meat pies at her shop in Bell Yard. The story first appeared in a serial entitled 'The String of Pearls' by Thomas Prest and was published in a magazine called *The People's Periodical* in 1846-7. The story was next published by Charles Fox in 1878, and has been used by countless authors since then. Both the story by Prest and the story by Fox say that the murders were committed in 1785.

Was Sweeney Todd a real person who actually murdered over a hundred victims who sat in his revolving chair; or was he just a figment of a writer's brilliant imagination?

SOURCE A

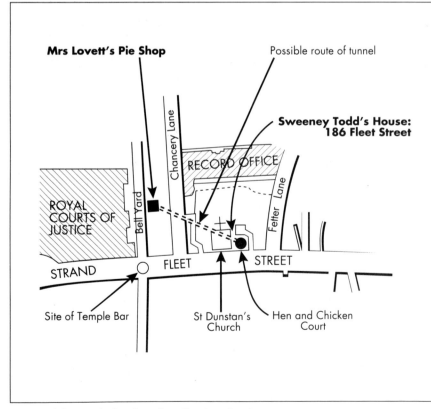

A map of the area in London where the story is set.

SOURCE B

'A horrid murder has been committed in Fleet Street on the person of a young gentleman from the country on a visit to his relatives in London. During the course of a walk through the city, he chanced to stop to admire the striking clock of St. Dunstan's Church, and there fell into conversation with a man in the clothing of a barber. The two men came to an argument, and, of a sudden, the barber took from his clothing a razor and slit the throat of the young man, thereafter disappearing into the alleyway of Hen and Chicken Court and was seen no more.'

From 'The Annual Register', a London newspaper, April 1785.

SOURCE C

'I did some research in the old street directories. Despite an exhaustive search through the directories of London through the years 1768 to 1850, I could find no Sweeney Todd.'

N. G. Lofts, a modern researcher, quoted in 'Sweeney Todd', by Peter Haining, 1979.

SOURCE D

'When I was a young Londoner I was shown in Fleet Street the very shop of the Demon Barber – and shuddered to think that meat pies were still on sale there.'

An extract from an historian of the theatre, from H. G. Hibbert's 'Playgoer's Memories', 1920.

SOURCE E

'I instituted a careful search of the vaults beneath St. Dunstan's Church, and I found a secret passage communicating with the cellar of the pie shop in Bell Yard, and afterwards I found a similar passage communicating with the cellar under Sweeney Todd's shop. Upon reaching the latter cellar, the first object that presented itself to me was a chair fixed to the roof by its legs. The plank on which this chair rested turned upon its centre, and could be made to turn by a simple contrivance above, so that any unfortunate person could be let down in a moment, and the vacant chair would come up and take the place of the one that had been above.'

An extract and illustration from the 1878 version of the story: 'Sweeney Todd, The Demon Barber of Fleet Street', 1878.

EXERCISE

1 Does Source A help you to decide whether Source B is true or not? Explain your answer.

2 How far does Source B make it seem likely that Sweeney Todd existed?

3 How far does Source E make it seem likely that Sweeney Todd existed?

4 Is Source D a primary or a secondary source? Explain your answer.

5 Do you think that H. G. Hibbert (Source D) had read Source E? Explain your answer.

6 Is it fair to assume that either H. G. Hibbert (Source D) or N. G. Lofts (Source C) was deliberately lying? Explain your answer.

7 Is Source B evidence that Sweeney Todd existed? Give reasons for your answer.

8 There is no legal record of any Sweeney Todd having been tried or convicted. Does this mean the story is untrue? Explain your answer.

9 What evidence would you look for to prove or disprove the story of Sweeney Todd? Give reasons for your answer.

3.2 MARY SEACOLE

In 1857 Mary Seacole wrote her life story, or autobiography. It was called *The Wonderful Adventures of Mrs Seacole*. In it she writes about her birth in Jamaica in 1801 and her trips to Panama and to England. She came to England in 1854 to offer her services as a nurse to Florence Nightingale. She was turned down. So she went to the Crimea on her own and set up a store where she cared for the sick and sold items to the soldiers. When the war ended she had to sell everything and return to England. She was unable to set herself up in business again and so became a bankrupt. To raise money she published her autobiography.

Examining the sources

Sources B – G are all different types of written sources. Make a list identifying all the different types of written sources and discuss the strengths and weaknesses that you think each one has. Then answer the questions.

Have your ideas about the strengths and weaknesses of each type of source changed?

The front cover of 'The Wonderful Adventures of Mrs Seacole', published in 1857.

SOURCE A

She describes how she decided to sail to England in order to go to the Crimea and help the soldiers. However, she was turned down by everybody that she went to for help to get to the Crimea. Finally:
'Once again, I tried and had an interview this time with one of Miss Nightingale's companions. She gave me the same reply and I read in her face the fact that had there had been a vacancy, I should not have been chosen to fill it. Was it possible that American prejudices against colour had some root here? Did these ladies shrink from accepting my aid because my blood flowed beneath a somewhat duskier skin than theirs? Tears streamed down my foolish cheeks, tears of grief that any should doubt my motives.'

An extract from 'The Wonderful Adventures'.

SOURCE B

Describing a typical day in her life in the Crimea:
'I was generally up and busy by daybreak, sometimes earlier. By seven o'clock in the morning coffee would be ready. From that time until nine, officers on duty in the neighbourhood, or passing by, would look in for breakfast, and about half past nine my sick patients began to show themselves. In the following hour they came thickly, and sometimes it was past twelve before I had got through the duty. That over, there was the hospital to visit across the way.'

An extract from 'The Wonderful Adventures'.

SOURCE C

'In the hour of their illness, these men, in common with many others, have found a kind and successful physician. Close to the railway Mrs Seacole, formerly of Kingston (Jamaica) and of several other parts of the world such as Panama, has pitched her abode – an iron storehouse with wooden sheds. Here she doctors and cures all manner of men with extraordinary success. She is always in attendance near the battlefield to aid the wounded, and has earned many a poor fellow's blessing.'

From an article in 'The Times', 27 September 1855. The article was written by William Russell, a war correspondant in the Crimea. It is his report of 14 September 1855.

SOURCE 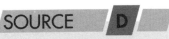 D

'Here I made the acquaintance of a celebrated person, Mrs Seacole, a coloured woman, who out of the goodness of her heart at her own expense supplied hot tea to the poor sufferers while they waited to be lifted into the boats [that took them to the hospital].'

'She did not spare herself if she could do any good to the suffering soldiers. In rain and snow, in storm and tempest, day after day, she was at her self chosen post with her stove and kettle, in any shelter she could find, brewing tea for all who wanted it, and there were many. Sometimes two hundred sick would be embarked on one day but Mrs Seacole was always equal to the occasion.'

From a letter by Dr Reid to his family, written in 1855 from Balaclava in the Crimea. Dr Reid was a surgeon with the British army.

SOURCE E

'I have seen her go down under fire with her little store of creature comforts for our wounded men. I saw her laden with wine and bandages and food for the wounded and prisoners. Her hut was surrounded every morning by men who had a faith in her proficiency [skill] in the healing art.'

From an article by William Russell published in 'The Times', 11 April 1857.

SOURCE F

'Dame Seacole was a kindly old soul,
And a kindly old soul was she
You might call for your pot, you might call for your pipe
In her tent on the Col so free.

She gave her aid to all who prayed
To hungry, and sick, and cold
Open hand and heart, alike ready to part
Kind words, and acts, and gold.

And now the good soul is in the hole
What redcoat in all the land,
But to set her upon her legs again
Will not lend her a willing hand?'

'col' = hill 'in the hole' = in trouble 'redcoat' = soldier

An extract from 'A Stir for Seacole'. This poem was published in 'Punch' on 6 December 1856.

EXERCISE

1 Look at Source B.
   What did Mary Seacole do between seven and nine o'clock in the morning when she was in the Crimea?

2 How do you think Mary Seacole felt about the events described in Source A?

3 Make a list of as many different ways an autobiography can be useful to a historian. Explain your answers fully.

4 Can Source C be used to support Source B? Explain your answer.

5 Why is Dr Reid's comment about Mary Seacole so useful as a source of information about her?

6 Look at Sources C and E. Both of these are written by William Russell. Source C was written at the time when the events happened. Does this mean it is more reliable than Source E, written two years later? Explain your answer.

7 'Poems are of little use because they only give you the attitudes and feelings of the person who wrote them.' With careful reference to Source F say whether you agree or disagree with this statement.

8 Mary Seacole excuses her vagueness about detail, saying: 'my memory is far from trustworthy and I kept no written diary.' How might this affect the way in which you would use the autobiography as a source of evidence? Explain your answer.

3.3 SCOTT AT THE SOUTH POLE

In 1911 two rival expeditions set out to reach the South Pole. Each of the men leading the expeditions wanted to be first to the Pole. The Norwegian team of four men, led by Roald Amundsen, left their base on 20 October. They reached the Pole on 15 December and by 26 January they had returned without losing a man. The fate of the British team, led by Captain Robert Scott, was very different. They reached the Pole on 17 January, over a month later than Amundsen, and all five of them died on the journey home. Why did the British expedition end so disastrously? Was it because of bad luck, or poor planning and organization?

To try and answer these questions it is important to first consider what conditions were like in the area around the South Pole. Both teams had to face the severe cold (always well below freezing point) and the snow blizzards which could make progress impossible for days. Both teams had to complete the 2253 km journey before the end of February when the Antarctic winter set in. Supplies were another problem. The necessary food and fuel could not be carried all the way, so it was stored at depots along each route. They also had to decide whether to walk and pull the sledges themselves, or use dogs and ponies.

Scott's team had to wait until the conditions were suitable for the ponies, and did not leave until 1 November. After tremendous difficulties they finally reached the Pole, but all five of them were suffering from frost bite, scurvy, hunger and exhaustion. By 19 March two of the team, Evans and Oates, had died and the remaining three men were trapped by a blizzard only 17 km from One Ton Depot (see map). They could go no further and died in their tent. Their bodies and their letters and diaries were found eight months later.

SOURCE A

At the South Pole!

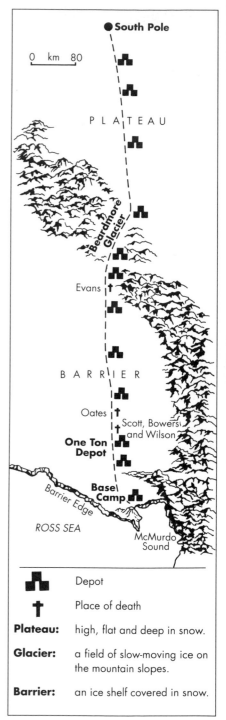

♣	Depot
†	Place of death
Plateau:	high, flat and deep in snow.
Glacier:	a field of slow-moving ice on the mountain slopes.
Barrier:	an ice shelf covered in snow.

The Polar journey.

SOURCE B

'We were ploughing along knee deep alternately hammering and encouraging our poor ponies. The ponies constantly collapsed and eventually we could only get them on for four or five metres at a time. Then we camped. Shot them all. Thank God the ponies are now done with and we begin the heavier work ourselves.'

An extract from the diary of one of Scott's team, 9 December, 1911.

SOURCE D

'The causes of the disaster are not due to faulty organization, but to bad luck. The weather throughout, stopped us. This cut into our supplies. Every detail of our food supplies, clothing and depots on the Plateau worked out to perfection. The Beardmore Glacier is not difficult in fine weather, but we did not get a single fine day. But no one in the world would have expected the temperatures which we encountered on the Barrier, $-30°$ F in the day, with continuous head-wind during our marches. We should have got through in spite of the weather but for the sickening of Oates, and a shortage of fuel in our depots, and finally, but for the storm which has fallen on us within 17 km of the depot. For four days we have been unable to leave the tent.'

'Message to the Public', written by Scott as he lay dying in his tent, March 1912.

SOURCE C

'Scott's team failed to make their distance because they became weak although they were eating their full rations. In the end they starved to death, their diet was seriously lacking in vitamins.'

An extract from 'The Worst Journey in the World' by Apsley Cherry-Garrard. He was a member of Scott's support party which did not go all the way to the Pole. Cherry-Garrard wrote the book in 1922.

SOURCE E

'Scott had based his plans on taking four men to the Pole. At the last moment he added a fifth and considerably increased the risks. Everything was arranged for four-man units: tents, gear, cookers, fuel and the depots along the route. After five days travel, Amundsen had travelled 225 km, and been pulled by the dogs all the way. Scott's men and ponies trudged eight hours to cover 21 km a day.'

Extracts from Roland Huntford's book 'Scott and Amundsen', 1979.

EXERCISE

1 Does Source A show Scott's or Amundsen's team at the South Pole? Give reasons for your answer.

2 What, according to Scott in Source D, was the most important reason for his expedition ending in disaster? Give reasons for your answer.

3 Huntford in Source E obviously disagrees with Scott. Do you agree that as Scott was there at the time his account must be the more reliable of the two? Give reasons for your answer.

4 In your opinion what was the most serious mistake made by Scott? Give reasons for your answer.

5 Did Scott's team fail because of bad luck, or because of bad planning and organization? Give reasons for your answer.

6 We have the diaries and letters written by members of Scott's team. These tell us what happened. Why then, do we need historians to write about the journey? Why not just read the diaries and letters?

3.4 THE TRENCHES

Propaganda and reality

Finding out what it was like in the trenches in the First World War is far from straightforward. Source material about the trenches has to be used carefully. Much of it was produced by the government and its supporters. They were worried about showing people how terrible conditions really were in case this stopped them from supporting the British war effort. Are the photographs from the Front and the accounts by the soldiers themselves any more reliable?

▲ 'The Surreys Play the Game!' A drawing of the first day of the Battle of the Somme. It appeared in British newspapers in July 1916. ('The Surreys' were the East Surrey Regiment.)

THE GAME

A company of the East Surrey Regiment is reported to have dribbled four footballs for a mile and a quarter into the enemy trenches.

On through the hail of slaughter
   Where gallant comrades fall,
Where blood is poured like water,
   They drive the trickling ball.
The fear of death before them
   Is but an empty name;
True to the land that bore them
   The Surreys play the game!

This poem was published in the 'Daily Mail' on 12 July 1916. It describes the first day of the Battle of the Somme. The poem was written by 'Touchstone', who worked for the 'Daily Mail'.

▼ A photograph of a German trench, 1917.

An advertisement published during the First World War.

'Let me make one thing clear. This is no fanciful story written miles behind the front. It is a true account as I saw it. We did not break any sporting records in a wild rush with flashing bayonets to get at the enemy. Nothing like the pictures in the illustrated magazines.

'Zero hour and we got out of the ditch and started to walk. Imagine us then rather like overladen porters going slow through a man-made thunderstorm.

'My plan was to walk alone and not get bunched up with the others. Frightened Germans with hands up and unarmed rose out of shellholes, two young soldiers turned and shot them. I kept walking about half a mile. I crawled into a big dugout. It was occupied by dead Germans. I had captured High Wood almost by myself. What I now had in mind was to go as quickly as possible in the opposite direction, as soon as possible. Leaving the dugout I ran for it.'

A first hand account of the first day of the Battle of the Somme written over sixty years later by the journalist B. A. Steward.

SOURCE

'The trenches were a morass of glue-like mud. We were among the ruins of the intense bombardment of ten days before. Concrete strong-posts were smashed; everywhere we looked we saw the mangled bodies of the dead. Floating on the surface of the flooded trench was the mask of a human face which had detached itself from the skull. I can remember a pair of hands which stuck out from the soaked soil like the roots of a tree turned upside down; one hand seemed to be pointing at the sky with an accusing gesture. Those fingers became an appeal to God in defiance of those who made the War.'

From 'Memoirs of an Infantry Officer' by Siegfried Sassoon. Sassoon fought in the trenches, but his experiences turned him against all war. He wrote his 'Memoirs' in the late 1920s.

EXERCISE

1 Source B is a photograph. Does this mean it is more reliable as evidence of the trenches than Source A? Give reasons for your answer.

2 Which Source do you think was more likely to be printed alongside Source A in British newspapers in 1916, Source C or Source E? Give reasons for your answer.

3 Do you think that the advertisement, Source D, was aimed at people in Britain or soldiers in the trenches? Give reasons for your answer.

4 Sources E and F are primary sources of evidence about the First World War. Source E was written sixty years after the war and Source F ten years after the war. How reliable are these sources?

5 Suggest possible reasons why Source D and Source F give different impressions of conditions in the trenches.

6 Do you think that people in Britain were misled about what it was really like in the trenches? Give reasons for your answer.

3.5 WHO SHOT THE RED BARON?

Baron von Richthofen was Germany's most successful pilot in the First World War. By 1918 he had shot down eighty enemy aircraft and was a national hero. The Allied soldiers nicknamed him the 'Red Baron'. Rivalry developed between the army and the air force and between the different nationalities on the Allied side, over who would be first to shoot him down.

On the morning of 21 April 1918, German planes, led by Richthofen, attacked British observation aircraft. The following events then took place:

1 Lieutenant Banks, a gunner in one of the British aircraft, fired at, and hit, one of the German planes.
2 More British aircraft, led by Captain Brown, joined in the fighting.
3 One of Brown's most inexperienced pilots, Lieutenant May, was chased along the valley of the River Somme by Richthofen.
4 Brown went to help May and fired a short burst as he flew across Richthofen's path.
5 May and Richthofen then flew over Morlancourt Ridge where Richthofen came under heavy fire from Sergeant Popkin, a machine gunner on the Ridge.
6 Richthofen then turned sharply to the east to return home, but his plane glided towards the ground and crashed.

Three men claimed to have shot Richthofen. They were:

Lieutenant Banks;
Captain Brown;
Sergeant Popkin.

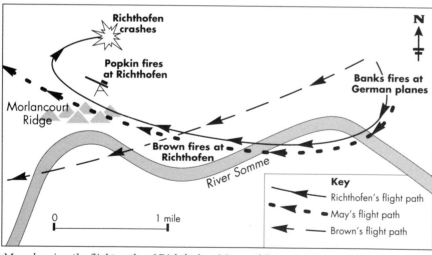

Map showing the flight paths of Richthofen, May and Brown.

SOURCE A

'Richthofen was not, and could not, have been shot from the air. No British plane, other than May's, was in sight at that time and May's guns could only fire forwards. This would have made it an impossibility as Richthofen was directly behind and slightly above May's plane.'

SOURCE B

'I kept dodging and spinning down until I ran out of sky and had to hedge-hop along the ground. Richthofen was continually firing. I didn't know what to do, I was a sitting duck. I felt he had me cold and I had to stop myself from ending it all by flying into the river. I was sure this was the end. Then as I looked around, I saw Richthofen do a spin and hit the ground. Looking up I saw Captain Brown's machine directly behind.'

Lieutenant May's account of what happened. May wrote this report as soon as he landed.

SOURCE C

'Richthofen started on a furious pursuit of one of the British planes. The plane which was accompanying the one under attack got above Richthofen. The three machines raced towards the British lines. Machine guns on the ground came into action against Richthofen who was also being fired on by both British planes. Suddenly his machine turned its nose downwards and crashed.'

From 'The New York Times', 24 April 1918.

◀ *From a report by R. H. Barron of the Royal Garrison Artillery. Barron was on Morlancourt Ridge at the time.*

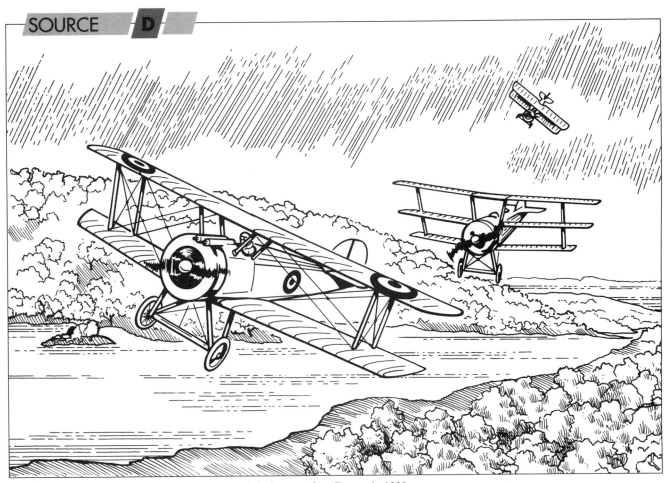

An artist's impression of the scene just before Richthofen was shot. Drawn in 1990.

SOURCE **E**

'We examined the body of Captain von Richthofen on the evening of 21 April. We found that he had one entrance and one exit wound caused by the same bullet. The gun firing this bullet must have been roughly level with Richthofen and fired from behind him. We are agreed that the wounds are such that they could not have been caused by fire from the ground.'

From a post mortem report on Richthofen's body, by two air force surgeons.

EXERCISE

1 How reliable do you think Lieutenant May's account is? (Source B.) Give reasons for your answer.

2 a In what ways do Sources A and C differ in their accounts of what happened?

b Suggest possible reasons why Sources A and C differ in their accounts of what happened.

3 'The artist of Source D must have based his drawing on Sources B and C.' Do you agree or disagree? Give reasons for your answer.

4 For each person – Lieutenant Banks, Captain Brown and Sergeant Popkin – explain:
a what evidence supports their claims to have shot Richthofen.
b what evidence contradicts their claims.

5 Is it possible to decide who shot Richthofen from the evidence here? Give reasons for your answer.

3.6 WOMEN AND THE FIRST WORLD WAR

The First World War was fought between August 1914 and November 1918. As the war began to involve more and more men, women did some of the jobs at home which, until that time, had always been done by men.

Before the war there had been many demonstrations by the **Suffragettes**, women who demanded the right to vote. During the war these demonstrations stopped. At the end of the war some women were given the right to vote. Most historians say that the First World War played a vital part in changing attitudes to women. This Unit looks at some of the evidence for this change in attitudes.

'For King and Country', by E. F. Skinner, c. 1917. Skinner was an official war artist.

A factory making ammunition, 1918.

SOURCE C

'At Greenwood and Batley's armament factory in Leeds, a girl, only 16 years of age, was injured at her machine. She had started at 6 a.m. Friday. With rests totalling two hours for meals on Friday, and half an hour for breakfast on Saturday, she kept on till the accident occurred at 7.30 a.m. Saturday. The women with her worked on for thirty one hours. When prosecuted, the factory manager said, by way of defence, that women subjected to this tremendous strain would earn between £1 and £2 a week. The magistrate, Horace Marshall, dismissed the case, saying: "the most important thing in the world today is that ammunition should be made." The senseless folly of this overwork was revealed when it was announced that 65,700 women had registered for war work, but only 1,250 of them had received employment.'

Sylvia Pankhurst, 'The Home Front', 1932. Sylvia Pankhurst had not supported the war. In 1915 she led an alternative to the 'Right to Serve' march, complaining that women who took over jobs once done by men were not paid the same wages as the men for the same jobs.

SOURCE D

'The idea of the WAACs is that they actually replace men. Each cook releases one man, while among the clerks at present there are four women to three men. Every WAAC who goes to France is like a pawn who gets to the top of the chess-board and is exchanged for a more valuable piece. She sends a fighting man to his job by taking all the jobs that are really women's after all. For is it not women's earliest job to look after man?'

The role of the Women's Army Auxiliary Corps (WAAC), from 'The Sword of Deborah', by F. Tennyson Jesse, 1918. This was an official book written for the Ministry of Information.

SOURCE E

Average weekly wages of women and girls in all industries

1906	64 p
December 1915	74$\frac{1}{2}$ p
December 1916	84 p
December 1917	£1.02 p
December 1918	£1.26$\frac{1}{2}$ p

EXERCISE

1 Do you think the artist of Source A was trying to give a realistic impression of an ammunition factory? Explain your answer.

2 Does Source C support the picture of ammunition factories given in Sources A and B? Give reasons for your answer.

3 Is Source C a primary or secondary source for a historian studying women during the First World War? Give reasons for your answer.

4 What attitude towards women did the author of Source D have?

5 Does Source E show that women were better off after the First World War? Give reasons for your answer.

6 Source D was also paid for by the government. It was intended to persuade women to join the WAAC. Does this mean historians studying attitudes to women at the time will not find it useful? Give reasons for your answer.

7 Do you think an historian studying women during the First World War will find Source A less useful than Source B? Explain your answer.

8 a Do the sources and text in this Unit show women's position in society was improved by the First World War? Explain your answer.

   b What other evidence would historians need to prove that women's position in society was improved by the First World War? Give reasons for your answer.

9 Are photographs, such as Source B, especially useful sources for historians? Explain your answer.

3.7 *LUSITANIA* SUNK: WHO WAS TO BLAME?

One of the most controversial incidents of the First World War occurred on 7 May 1915, when the British passenger liner *Lusitania* was sunk by a German submarine off the Irish coast, during a voyage from New York to Liverpool. Over one thousand people lost their lives. The submarine sank the *Lusitania* without warning, apparently ignoring the normal practice of allowing the crew and passengers to escape into their lifeboats before their ship was sunk. The sinking led to a public outcry in America because some of the dead were Americans. Despite attempts by both Germany and Britain to persuade America to enter the war on their side, it remained neutral. America sold crucial supplies of food and armaments to both sides, but American law did not allow weapons or ammunition to be sent on passenger ships as this would put the lives of the passengers in danger. The British government blamed the sinking on German 'barbarism', but the German government blamed the British for the tragedy.

SOURCE A

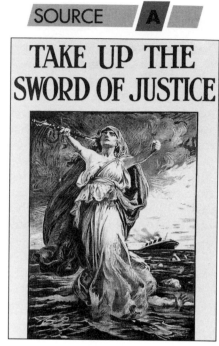

A British poster showing the sinking of the 'Lusitania', published in 1915.

SOURCE B

A drawing of the sinking of the 'Lusitania', published in the 'Illustrated London News', 1915.

SOURCE C

'Prior to the *Lusitania* leaving New York, threatening statements were published in the American press by German authorities foretelling the sinking of the liner. Without any warning she was struck by a torpedo between the third and fourth funnels. There was evidence that a second, and perhaps a third torpedo was fired, and the great ship sank within twenty minutes.'

'This is the foulest act of wilful murder ever committed on the high seas. It was only to be expected that the enemy would attempt to justify its evil work by proclaiming that the vessel was armed. The *Lusitania* was never actually in Government service. Another German lie exposed!'

An extract from a booklet published by the Cunard Company in October 1915.

SOURCE D

'The German Ambassador warned Americans against sailing on the *Lusitania*. Does a pirate act thus? Does he take pains to save human lives?'

'Nobody regrets more than we Germans the hard necessity of sending to their deaths hundreds of men. Yet the sinking was a justifiable act of war just like the bombarding of a fortress. The sinking was a military necessity not only because she was equipped for fighting, but especially because we had to protect our brave soldiers from death and destruction by American munitions of war.'

A statement issued by Baron Von Schwarzenstein, an official of the German government. It was published in the 'Washington Post', an American newspaper, 13 May 1915.

SOURCE E

'Under strict secrecy the *Lusitania* entered dry-dock on 12 May 1913. Special shell racking was installed, revolving gun-rings were mounted on the rear deck so that it could mount two six-inch guns. Other decks were adapted to take four six-inch guns on either side.

'War was declared on 4 August, by 8 August the *Lusitania* was in dry-dock again to have her guns installed. On 17 September she was registered by the Admiralty as an armed auxiliary cruiser.'

Adapted from 'Lusitania' by Colin Simpson, published in 1972. He came to his conclusions about the alterations to the 'Lusitania' after studying the original working drawings.

SOURCE F

'We need to entangle neutral ships with the German submarines, and the ships we most need to involve are the Americans'.'

From a letter in 1914 from Winston Churchill, the government minister in charge of the British Admiralty, to Walter Runciman at the Board of Trade.

EXERCISE

1 What is the poster, Source A, asking people to do?

2 Which Source, A or B, would be more useful to the historian? Give reasons for your answer.

3 How far do Sources C and D disagree? Support your answer with reference to the sources.

4 Suggest possible reasons why Sources C and D disagree.

5 Does the fact that they disagree mean that one of them must be wrong? Give reasons for your answer.

6 Read Source E and then go back and study Source B again. Source B does not show any of the alterations described in Source E. Does this mean that the alterations were never actually carried out? Give reasons for your answer.

7 Is there enough evidence here to prove who was to blame for the sinking of the *Lusitania*? Give reasons for your answer.

3.8 UNEMPLOYMENT IN THE 1930s

The 1930s brought serious unemployment to Britain. From 1930 to 1935 there were over two million unemployed and many people were out of work for most of the 1930s. Places with older industries, such as coal, cotton and ship-building were hit hardest. Many people called this time **The Depression**.

Payment of unemployment benefit was extended to cover most working people in 1921. However, the system did not work well and by the 1930s 'dole' payments (as such unemployment benefit was called) were very low. Not all parts of Britain were severely hit by unemployment. Efforts were made by journalists, writers and photographers to explain to people in other parts of the country what unemployment was like. In this Unit we will try to find out what it was like to be unemployed in Britain fifty years ago.

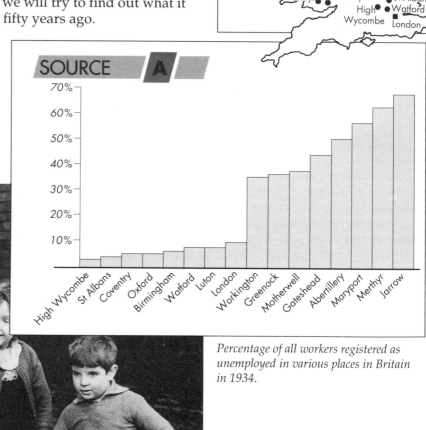

SOURCE A

Percentage of all workers registered as unemployed in various places in Britain in 1934.

SOURCE B

A photograph of an unemployed man taken in 1939.

SOURCE C

'If only he had work. Just imagine what it would like. On the whole my husband has worked about one year out of twelve and a half. His face was lovely when I married him, but now he's skin and bones. When I married he was robust and he had a good job. He was earning from eight pounds to ten pounds a week. He's a left-handed ship's riveter – a craft which should be earning him a lot of money. He fell out of work about four months after I was married, so I've hardly known what a week's wage was.'

Oral evidence collected by Felix Greene in 1935 from a ship-builder's wife.

SOURCE D

	p
Rent	43
Coal	17.5
Gas	12.5
Union and Insurance subscriptions	16
Savings Club	5
Meat	10
Milk	12.5
Bread	23.5
Margarine	10
Jam	4
Clog Irons*	2.5
	£1.56.5

* For re-soling clogs - clogs were boots worn by working people in Lancashire at the time.

Weekly spending of unemployed mill-worker's family in Lancashire, 1931. Their income from the dole was £1.59p.

SOURCE E

'When a man fell out of work he would, on the first day, dress in his Sunday suit with collar and tie. He shaved, pinned on his ex-serviceman's badge and, head held high, lined up at the labour exchange. He kept up his spirits by joking with his mates, the whole works or coal mine having shut down at once. As the weeks passed, the unemployed man changed. He stopped dressing up. He acquired a slouch, the result of hanging around street corners with his hands in his pockets. As the alternative to standing in the street, he might shuffle into the library reading room to look at magazine pictures of society beauties.'

From an article in the 'Observer' newspaper, 6 February 1966 about the 1930s.

EXERCISE

1 Study Source A and the map. What do these sources tell you about unemployment in Britain in the 1930s?

2 Study Source B. What does this source tell you about unemployment which you cannot tell from Source A?

3 Study Source C.
  a This is oral evidence collected by Felix Greene for his book. How is it useful to you in your study of unemployment in the 1930s?
  b In what ways would you need to be careful before relying on oral evidence such as this?

4 Study Source E.
  a This journalist probably did some research into the conditions of the unemployed. Which of Sources A to C does the journalist seem to have used? Explain your selection.
  b How useful is Source E in your study of unemployment in the 1930s? Explain your answer.

5 Study Sources B and D.
  a Does Source D support the statement that the dole was not enough to live on? Explain your answer.
  b The three people in Source B do not appear to be hungry. Does this prove that the dole must have been enough to live on? Explain your answer.

6 a Study Source C. State whether it contains:
    i only facts,
    or ii only opinions,
    or iii facts and opinions.
    Give reasons for your choice.

  b Study Source E. State whether it contains:
    i only facts,
    or ii only opinions,
    or iii facts and opinions.
    Give reasons for your choice.

7 If you were writing a propaganda pamphlet about the miseries of unemployment in the 1930s which two of Sources A, B, C, D or E would you include in it? Explain how you would use them.

3.9 STALIN: MAN OR MYTH?

Joseph Stalin is one of the most important figures in the history of twentieth-century Russia. He was born in 1879. When he was young he had a severe attack of smallpox which left his face deeply pitted. Another illness left his left arm a few inches shorter than his right arm. Between 1900 and 1913 he organized strikes and robbed banks. He was captured and imprisoned but escaped three times. From 1913 to 1917 he was imprisoned in Siberia.

In 1917 he returned from Siberia to take part in the revolution which ended the rule of the Tsar and led to a Communist government. In 1924 Stalin gained control of the Communist Party and became ruler of the Soviet Union. His harsh industrial and agricultural policies made him many enemies. At the same time, efforts were made to increase his popularity and prestige. Many people came to see Stalin as a god-like figure.

Anyone trying to find out about Stalin has to be able to separate the man from the myth. In order to do this, you have to understand how the myth was created.

Examining the sources

All the sources given here are pictures. Two are photographs and one is a painting. Before answering the questions, discuss the advantages and disadvantages of paintings and photographs as sources of evidence. Now answer the questions. How far are your ideas about the advantages and disadvantages of pictures as sources of evidence supported by these three sources?

SOURCE **A**

Stalin's record card and photograph from police files, 1912-13.

SOURCE **B**

Stalin congratulating the wives of army officers, taken in 1937.

Stalin, the schoolboy, is the one leading the group and waving his cap. Stalin ordered this picture to be painted when he was ruling the Soviet Union in the 1930s.

EXERCISE

1 Look at the text. What physical defects did Stalin have?

2 Look at Source A.
   a This is a police photograph. Why do you think it was taken?
   b Does your answer to **a**, about the purpose of the source, help you to decide how reliable this source might be as a picture of Stalin?

3 Look at Sources A and B. What lessons can be learnt about using photographs as sources of evidence?

4 Look at Source B.
   a This is an official photograph of Stalin. What impression of Stalin is it meant to give?
   b Which one of these statements do you agree with:
   ● This source is unreliable.
   ● This source is a reliable source of evidence of the image Stalin wished to create.
   ● This is a reliable source of evidence of what Stalin was like.
   Give reasons for your answer.

5 Look at Source C.
   a What do you think Stalin wanted this picture to show?
   b What did he not want the picture to show?
   c Has this picture any value as a source of evidence about:
   ● Stalin's childhood?
   ● Stalin's character?
   Give reasons for your answers.

3.10 GUERNICA

Background information
In 1936 a Civil War began in Spain with a revolt by Fascist army officers, led by General Franco, against the Republican government. Franco and the Fascists were helped by troops and planes from the other Fascist countries of Europe – Hitler's Germany and Mussolini's Italy. Guernica was a town in the Basque region of Spain which was famous for its historic and religious importance. During the Civil War it was in a Republican area, which was attacked and captured by the Fascists. Guernica was almost totally destroyed on 26 April 1937. The Republicans said that Guernica had been bombed and machine gunned by German planes fighting for Franco and the Fascists. The Fascists denied the bombing story, and said the town had been blown up and burnt by retreating Republican troops. This Unit looks at some of the sources that can be used as evidence to decide what happened in Guernica.

SOURCE **B**

'On 27 April a Fascist spokesman said that the Basques had destroyed Guernica. The next day the Fascists solemnly announced that none of their aircraft had left the ground on 27 April. On 28 April the Fascists captured Guernica. Foreign journalists with the Fascist army were told that, while a 'few bomb fragments' had been found in Guernica most of the damage had been caused by Basques, presumably to inspire indignation against the Fascists.'

From Hugh Thomas, 'The Spanish Civil War', 1961.

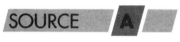

SOURCE **A**

The ruins of Guernica.

SOURCE C

A photograph which the Roman Catholic priest of Guernica said he took of the bombing raid.

SOURCE D

'I walked through the still-burning town. Hundreds of bodies had been found in the debris. Most were charred beyond recognition. At least two hundred others were riddled with machine-gun bullets as they fled to the hills.'

'Daily Express', April 1937.

EXERCISE

1 What does Source A prove? Give reasons for your answer.

2 Does Source A Confirm or contradict Source B? Explain your answer.

3 Is there any reason to suspect the spokesman quoted in Source B might not be reliable? Give reasons for youranswer.

4 When do you think the journalist in Source D visited Guernica? Give reasons for your answer.

5 Is Source C reliable as evidence of what happened to Guernica?

6 Some German pilots later suggested they were trying to bomb a bridge outside Guernica but they missed.
   a Does this help you decide how reliable the statements of the Fascist spokesman in Source B are? Explain your answer.
   b Considering the sources here do you think this is a likely explanation?

7 What do you think happened in Guernica? Give reasons for your answer.

8 Why are historians so interested in knowing where their sources come from?

3.11 LONDON AND THE BLITZ

From early in 1939 it was clear that war was likely to start soon. The government expected massive air raids on British cities. It was feared that millions of people would be killed and that the raids would cause chaos, making it impossible for Britain to go on fighting. Plans were made to build shelters and to move children to country areas. This was called evacuation.

War broke out in September 1939. After the Battle of Britain in August 1940, Hitler ordered the bombing of British cities. The first raids on London were in September 1940, and by the end of that year 13,000 tons of bombs had been dropped on the city. Other cities were also bombed. This was known as The Blitz.

These sources look at some of the things the people of London did during The Blitz. In a serious crisis, like a war, the government had to play a much bigger part in people's lives. These sources also look at how the government handled this task.

SOURCE **C**

SOURCE **A**

Photograph taken in Piccadilly underground station in 1940.

SOURCE **B**

'East London paused for a moment yesterday to lick its wounds after what had been planned by Hitler as a night of terror. But it carried on.

'During a five hour tour of the bombed area, I met only one person who was fed up – a youth who complained that there were not enough shelters.'

Extract from an article in the 'Daily Herald', 9 September 1940.

SOURCE **D**

WAR EMERGENCY

UNDERGROUND STATIONS MUST NOT BE USED AS AIR RAID SHELTERS

The public are informed that in order to operate the Railways for essential movement, Underground Stations cannot be used as air raid shelters. In any event a number of stations would have to be cleared for safety in certain contingencies

UNDERGROUND

London transport poster from 1939.

Photograph taken on 9 September, 1940 showing damaged houses in Stepney, London.

'The press versions of life going on normally in the East End are greatly distorted. There was no bread, no electricity, no gas, no milk, no telephones. There was thus every excuse for people to be distressed. There was no understanding in the huge government buildings of central London for the tiny crumbled streets of massed populations.'

Extract from an eyewitness report, September 1940.

EXERCISE

1 Study Sources A and D.
   a In what ways do these sources seem to contradict each other?
   b The government was worried that if it allowed the underground stations to be used as shelters, people would stay down there and never come out. Why didn't they say this in Source D?
   c In fact when The Blitz started, many people began to use the stations as shelters and soon the officials did not try to stop them. Why do you think this was?

2 Study Source C. This photograph was censored by the government. Suggest reasons why the government did not want it to be published.

3 Study Sources B and E.
   a What impression of the effects of The Blitz was the *Daily Herald* trying to give?
   b Suggest reasons why it was trying to give this impression.
   c What is the attitude of the writer of Source E towards the government?
   d Both Sources B and E are primary sources of evidence about The Blitz, yet they give different impressions of it. Suggest reasons for this.

4 a Choose three of the Sources in this Unit which you think are the most useful sources of evidence about The Blitz. Explain your choice.
   b If you were trying to write a history of The Blitz and of its impact on the lives of ordinary people, what other sorts of evidence would be available to you?
   c When your research was finished, how accurate an account do you think would be possible?

3.12 THE DEATH OF HITLER

Background information

Adolf Hitler (born in 1889), the leader of the Nazi party, was Führer of Germany between 1933 and 1945. His desire to conquer land for Germany led to the outbreak of the Second World War in 1939. By 1942, after a series of military victories, Hitler and the Nazis ruled most of Europe and North Africa. By 1945, however, they were facing defeat as British, French and American forces attacked Germany from the west, and the Russian army invaded from the east. On 21 April 1945 the Russians entered the outskirts of Berlin (the German capital). Having totally surrounded the city they finally captured it on 2 May. Germany surrendered on 7 May. But what happened to Hitler?

Hitler was last heard of at the end of April, hiding in his underground bunker next to the Chancellery building in Berlin with a few of his closest officials and servants. Soon rumours began to spread – some said Hitler had died fighting in Berlin, others said he had escaped, possibly to South America. One thing does seem to be certain – Hitler has not been seen alive since the end of April 1945. Did Hitler die in April/May 1945? If so, how did he die and what happened to his body?

> **People**
>
> **Arthur Axmann** Leader of the Hitler Youth. He was arrested by British and American soldiers in December 1945.
>
> **Admiral Doenitz** The new ruler of Germany after Hitler's death. He had left Berlin on 21 April.
>
> **Goebbels** One of Hitler's most trusted assistants. Responsible for propaganda.
>
> **Heinz Linge** Hitler's servant in 1945. In May 1945 he was captured by the Russians; he remained a prisoner of the Russians until 1955.
>
> **Marshal Zhukov** Commander of the Russian army which captured Berlin.

SOURCE A

'German men and women, soldiers of the German army, our Führer, Adolf Hitler has fallen. At the end of his struggle he met a hero's death in the capital of the German Reich.'

A radio broadcast by Admiral Doenitz on 1 May 1945.

SOURCE B

GRAND ADMIRAL DOENITZ
MOST SECRET   URGENT   OFFICER ONLY
1 MAY

THE FUHRER DIED YESTERDAY. HIS WILL OF 29 APRIL APPOINTS YOU AS REICH PRESIDENT. TIME AND FORM OF ANNOUNCEMENT TO THE PRESS AND TO THE TROOPS IS LEFT TO YOU.
CONFIRM RECEIPT.

GOEBBELS

A telegram found in Admiral Doenitz's papers by American soldiers after Doenitz was captured.

SOURCE C

'There almost upright in a sitting position on a couch was the body of Adolf Hitler. A small hole showed on his right temple and a trickle of blood ran slowly down his cheek. One pistol, a Walther 7.65, lay on the floor where it had dropped from his right hand.'

Heinz Linge, interviewed by an English newspaper in 1955.

SOURCE D

'As we entered we saw the Führer sitting on a small divan. The Führer was only slightly slumped forward and everyone recognised that he was dead. His jaw hung somewhat loosely down and a pistol lay on the floor. Blood was dripping from both temples, and his mouth was bloody and smeared, but there was not much blood smattered about. I believe that Hitler took poison first and then shot himself through the mouth.'

Part of a statement made by Arthur Axmann shortly after his capture.

SOURCE E

In 1968 the Russian government published a book called *The Death of Adolf Hitler*. The book contained a number of documents:

- A report written by a Russian soldier in which he claimed to have found a badly burned copse in the garden of the Chancellery building on 5 May 1945.
- A photograph of the body (see below).
- A report written by Russian scientists after they had examined the body on 8 May, part of which is printed below.
- An interview with a Russian officer who stated that Hitler's dentist had confirmed the body was Hitler's on 9 May.

The photograph from the book.

The remains of a male corpse disfigured by fire were delivered in a wooden box.

The body
Since the body parts are heavily charred it is impossible to describe the features of the dead man. But the following could be established:
a Stature: about 165 cm.
b Age: somewhere between 50 and 60 years.
c The most important anatomical finding for identification of the person are the teeth.
d Part of the skull is missing.

Cause of death
On the body, considerably damaged by fire, no visible signs of severe injuries or illnesses could be detected. The presence in the mouth of the remains of a crushed glass container and the marked smell of bitter almonds coming from the body, and the forensic chemical test which established the presence of the cyanide compounds, permit the commission to arrive at the conclusion that death was caused by poisoning with cyanide.

Extracts of the report written by the scientists after they had investigated the body.

EXERCISE

1 a What impression does Admiral Doenitz give of the way in which Hitler died in Source A?
b Why do you think Doenitz might have done this? Explain your answer.

2 Which would you consider to be the more reliable source, Source A or Source B? Give reasons for your answer.

3 Both Linge (Source C) and Axmann (Source D) were reporting what they had seen. Does this mean their evidence must be true? Explain your answer.

4 Is Source E a primary or a secondary source? Explain your answer.

5 Do you think the conclusion of the Russian scientists in Source E ('death was caused by poisoning with cyanide') is supported by the evidence? Explain your answer.

6 Why do you think Sources C, D and E give different accounts of Hitler's death?

7 Do you think it is possible to say what happened to Hitler on the basis of the sources here? Explain your answer.

8 'The closer a source is to the time the event happened, the more accurate it is.' Do you agree or disagree with this statement? Give reasons for your answer.

9 Is it important for people to know, with complete accuracy, what happened in the past? Explain your answer.